Places in the World

by Arlene Block

PEARSON

Scott
Foresman

What You Already Know

Weather is what it is like outside. Weather changes from day to day. It can be hot or cold. It can be wet or dry. The wind can blow. There can be clouds. The Sun can shine. Weather can be measured with tools. A thermometer is a weather tool. It measures the temperature. It tells how hot or cold something is.

Different clouds bring different kinds of weather. Water vapor is a kind of water in the air. Clouds form when water vapor cools. Rain, sleet, and snow are kinds of wet weather.

Seasons are times of the year. Seasons happen in a pattern. Weather changes during the year. In some places weather changes a lot during the seasons.

What if you are going on a trip? Should you pack a T-shirt or a warm coat? In this book you will find out what it is like in different places in the world.

Wear warm clothes if you visit somewhere snowy.

Changing Seasons

Some places are always hot. Some places are always cold. Some places have temperatures that change. They have four different seasons. It is cold and snowy in winter. It is warm in spring. It is hot in summer. It is cool in fall.

Squirrel

Many plants can live with season changes. Some trees change with the seasons. Their leaves turn colors in the fall. Then the leaves drop. New leaves grow in the spring.

Animals can live with the season changes too. Squirrels store food when it is warm. Then they are ready for the winter.

Mountain Places

In places with mountains the air stays cool most of the year. The temperature can be very cold on mountaintops. Some of the peaks, or tops, have snow and ice all year. It is too cold for trees or plants to grow there. It is not as cold at the bottom. Plants and trees grow near the bottoms of mountains.

Mountain goat

The body parts of some animals help them live on mountains. Mountain goats live on mountains. They have hooves (huvz). Their hooves help them climb and jump from rock to rock. Their thick fur coats keep them warm.

Many people like to ski on snowy mountains.

Desert Places

You will not get wet in a desert. Deserts are very dry. They do not get much rain. The Sun shines on most days. The temperature can be very hot. There are not many clouds.

The temperature drops at night. It gets much colder.

Scorpion

Many plants and animals live in deserts. The scorpion sleeps under a rock in the day. It is cool and shady under the rock. At night the scorpion comes out to look for food.

Cactus plants

Desert plants do not need much water. Many different cactus plants live in deserts. They can store water for a long time.

Strong winds blow sand into piles called dunes.

Tropical Places

Leave your warm coat at home if you go to a tropical place! The air there stays warm all year. It is warm in the day and at night. Tropical places are the warmest places in the world. There is a lot of rain. Most rain forests and some beaches are tropical places.

Chameleon

Different plants and animals live in rain forests. Many plants grow well where it is warm and wet. These plants are food for many kinds of animals. Some animals, such as chameleons, live in the trees. Other animals live on the ground.

Many people enjoy tropical beaches.

Polar Places

What are the coldest places on Earth? Polar places! It is very cold in these places most of the year. Snow and ice cover the ground. Huge blocks of ice float in the water. Very little sun shines in the winter.

It is hard for living things to be where it is so cold. Not many people live in polar places.

Some people live in polar places all year.

People in polar places need to wear clothes that keep them warm. Only a few plants can grow.

Some animals live in polar places. Penguins live in polar places all year. Their fat helps keep them warm. They also have thick coats of feathers.

Penguins live in polar places.

Many Places

It is different in different places in the world. There are four different seasons in some places. Mountain places are cool most of the year. Deserts are dry. Tropical places are hot and wet all year.

Changing seasons   **Mountain**   **Desert**

Polar places are the coldest places on Earth. They are cold and icy all year long.

Different places have different plants and animals. Some animals have special body parts that help them where they live.

People live in different places too. What is it like where you live?

Tropical　　　　　**Polar**

Glossary

beaches   sandy land next to water

hooves   hard parts on the feet of some animals

peaks   the pointed tops of mountains

polar   very cold

tropical   hot and wet